ROAD SERIES

Relishing each step as we journey to
our destination

Collins Nwosu

WESTBOW·
PRESS
A DIVISION OF THOMAS NELSON
& ZONDERVAN

Scriptures taken from the Holy Bible, New International Version®, NIV®. Copyright © 1973, 1978, 1984, 2011 by Biblica, Inc.™ Used by permission of Zondervan. All rights reserved worldwide. www.zondervan.com The "NIV" and "New International Version" are trademarks registered in the United States Patent and Trademark Office by Biblica, Inc.™ All rights reserved.

WestBow Press books may be ordered through booksellers or by contacting:

WestBow Press
A Division of Thomas Nelson & Zondervan
1663 Liberty Drive
Bloomington, IN 47403
www.westbowpress.com
1 (866) 928-1240

ISBN: 978-1-4908-4627-9 (sc)
ISBN: 978-1-4908-4628-6 (e)

Library of Congress Control Number: 2014913413

Printed in the United States of America.

WestBow Press rev. date: 8/18/2014

CONTENTS

Dedication...vii

Epigraph viii

Foreword... ix

Preface.. xi

Acknowledgment...xiii

1.   Follow...1

2.   Abundance, Lack, Commonplace, Scarce..................5

3.   The Subway, Maps and Direction................................7

4.   Traffic Lights, Moving with God and
      Not The Crowd 9

5.   Business Class 13

6.   Exercise Your Faith – Don't Limit God.................... 17

7.   I want to Enjoy Being in God's Presence
      and Not Just Enter it Out of a Sense of
      Duty or Discipline.. 21

8.   Trust – Give In – Let Go 23

9.   Ask and You Shall Have It...25

10.   Pay the Price 29

11.   Can you Give What You Do not Have? 31

12.   I'm Sane, They Know Nothing 35

13. Watch Forward 37

14. Take Heed, Stay Sharp, Stay Alive 41

15. You Mean He Did that with My Gift? 43

16. I Trust God But...? 45

17. Makurdi-Obollo-Awka 47

18. A Living Bible 49

19. Light On A Hill 51

20. Gaze Upon...More and Be Taken in 55

21. Rock the Boat 57

22. Getting Ahead, A Roundabout 59

23. Going on Everyone Else's Assumption 61

24. He Said... Just Do It 63

25. Satellite Navigation 65

About the Author 67

Notes 69

DEDICATION

This is dedicated to God, and to You.

"Not all those who wander are lost."

-J.R.R. Tolkein

FOREWORD

One of the most profound, most popular imageries of the Christian life is that of a way. We are on our way to heaven. Jesus Christ our Lord says of Himself: "I am the *Way*, the Truth and the Life." In the Acts of the Apostles also, the Church, the assembly of believers, is called the Way. The Christian is on a journey, a journey to Eternity.

In these pages, we see the sojourns of a wayfarer – a wayfarer here on earth, and on the road to eternity – and how every tiny, apparently insignificant occurrence in life's journey is woven into the grand theme of a Christian's journey into his final destination: heaven, for, when we have traversed this terrain called earth, there is a heavenly home waiting for us at the end of the journey. This home – if we have lost or missed anything as we journey through this world – is one we cannot afford to miss. The disaster of missing it is as unbearable as it cannot be remedied.

God speaks to us in different ways: in scripture, revelations, through the direction of our God-fearing leaders, and so on. He also speaks to us through the events of our daily lives. And IT TAKES A SENSITIVE SPIRIT TO RECOGNISE THE VOICE OF THE LORD in the noise that characterizes our daily lives. But listen we must, if we must grow and know what God is saying in these circumstances. And here lies the value of this book; beyond what is written in these pages, it invites us to listen to God in every situation, and to see the passing events of this life from the perspective of the unchanging reality of God's heavenly kingdom.

I commend our brother's sensitivity, and I recommend this book to everyone who wants to pick God's signals in the ordinary events of this life.

Reverend Fr Rahapael Fabgohun

PREFACE

2010 April
IT'S BEGINING

For a while now I have tried to put to paper my life experience. Suffice it to say that when we use the expression "Life is a journey" or "...move along life's road", little do we know how apt we are. Allow me to draw analogies from real travel experiences on the road, in the air, on water and at home, and to relate them to our lives. You may personalize it as you journey along these pages because I believe you will find an experience or more that you could relate to.

Recently I was travelling to Kaduna through the Keffi-Kwoi-Kachia route and was speeding up. My focus was on the road while my heart was at my destination, home to my wife and kids. Suddenly, the sun came out from behind the clouds. It was as if the heavenly curtains had been pulled and there it was, the majestic rays pouring unto the countryside. I seemed to notice for the first time the lush green meadows that stretched for kilometers on end. There in the fields were wild flowers in all their glory, bathing in the golden rays of the sun. The hills were not left out as they overlooked the plains, bathing in the sun, an array of powerful and rugged beauty.

In that moment I became acutely aware of my surroundings as I zoomed past. It seemed I had just been liberated from my destination mentality. I was soaking up the journey as well. I would get home tired after the long drive, but will I just crumple up in bed and ask not to be disturbed until the next day? Or would I also begin to enjoy my family, allowing them tumble over a tired man, recognizing their love above my fatigued body? After all, they were the reason I was on that journey to Kaduna in the first place.

For you, it might be something else that you've taken for granted. It may be the gift of sleep, sight, taste, smell, parents, siblings, your job, God...you name it. You simply need to begin to take it all in, each breath, each step, a smile, a hug and so forth. He did give us all things to enjoy[1]. Once again I encourage you to make each story yours.

---

[1] 1 Timothy 6:17

ACKNOWLEDGMENT

I thank God for making me a part of this write up. I am also grateful to Priscilla, my wife, who encouraged me to keep at it. Fr Ralph, you prompted me to collate this into much more than just a periodic article. Your love and support is most appreciated. Kolade Ajila, you have a gift for fine detail, thank you for editing this work. Tadd Butler, Cherry Calvin, your consistent yet gentle follow ups have been invaluable to seeing this journey come through, thank you all.

19 July, 2013

FOLLOW

I had just left my wife and daughter to head home while I drove to the office. As I drove behind them, it occurred to me to buy them lunch since she had spent a good portion of the day at the hospital and would be tired after the long drive home. She was six months pregnant, by the way. So I sped up, rolled up beside her and signaled her to follow me. She understood and fell in behind my vehicle.

A short while later, we arrived at an intersection which could go right, left of straight, and she drove ahead of my car at that point. "What are you doing, baby? Do you know where I am taking you to? What if you go straight when we are meant to go left? At least I'm heading left?" All these thoughts ran through my mind. It was soon our turn to move and she sped off! Her car was nowhere in sight. I drove straight on, hoping she'd be sensitive enough to realize I was meant to be leading, and she to follow. I knew the destination and all she had was a hint that following me was for good.

I caught up with her; she had slowed down but was almost missing it again. Well, she followed this time and I led her to the hotel to have a buffet lunch with the child.

Now it struck me! Jesus asks us to follow him.[2][3] He is the Good Shepherd who knows where the pastures are. The road we know might be too long or outright wrong. But we often do not follow. We do our own thing often and miss the way. Worse than that, we miss our destiny. Following is quite active. Imagine that I had gone right and my wife went straight? Just think for a moment that, although there was another route ahead to take us to the buffet had she not slowed down and continued on her way, what would have been the outcome. And it goes on and on.

Christ has called us to follow. We should do just that. If we have missed it we should simply stop where we are and turn back to him. If we don't know the way back, we should call on him from our hearts, and he'll come up (catch up) with us and lead us aright. It may be a longer

---

[2]   Luke 9:23

[3]   John 14:6

route this time but it will ultimately lead to the buffet. And what buffet? Not a passing one, but the banquet of eternal life.

Can you relate to this road experience? Personalize it and see where it takes you!

28 – 30 July, 2012

ABUNDANCE, LACK, COMMONPLACE, SCARCE

We had a vision – well, I did – of a car for our house. While praying I had asked God for a new household vehicle for my wife. The Holy Spirit then led me to ask for a specific brand of vehicle. In addition, I was led to visualize the specification and color. Wow! It was awesome because I could see a metallic black Mercedes Vito with alloy wheels and factory-tinted glasses. Immediately after the prayer session, I informed my wife and family of the vision. To make it real they all began looking out for the vehicle to visualize it and exercise our faith.

Now my wife and I had won a raffle draw star prize by VISA to attend the opening ceremony of the London 2012 Olympics (We'll get into this another day). We settled into our hotel nicely and the next day took a stroll along Edgware Road. Bam! There it was, the Mercedes Vito. Oh, here comes another one and another one and another.... Oh boy! Here goes one that looks like it, the Mercedes Viano. Guess what? While the vehicle was scarce in Nigeria, it was abundantly present in London. Not only was it a common sight, it was serving mainly as a taxi. I exclaimed: our vision car was commonplace here!

Then the Holy Spirit told me that what was scarce anywhere was abundant in God's presence. Whatever was out of reach for us was within reach for God. All we have to do is remain connected in Him and to Him: simply being in right standing and holding on to Him. One other thing that struck me was that, while these blessings and abundance were commonplace with God, we should not take them for granted. Once you leave 'London' for 'Nigeria', the abundance will cease and commonplace becomes a privilege and struggle.

So we were to remain the 'London' of God's presence and will always. It is not to our benefit to leave for any reason. Abide in me and bear fruit... much fruit, He tells us.[4]

---

4 John 15:4,5

30 July, 2012

THE SUBWAY, MAPS AND DIRECTION

My Wife and I needed to get to Canada Water and we had to keep making calls, consulting the map and following instructions until we arrived at our destination. We had to walk from the hotel, take a train ride and walk from the train station to meet out our host. At a point during the walk before we met Mr B (not his real name), he had directed that we turn left and keep walking down. We assumed it was our left but later came to discover it was *his* own left (how were we to know?) But we kept in touch with him until we met up. He was such a wonderful host who made us comfortable, and so on; it was all worth it in the end.

Just imagine that we did not consult the maps, make the calls and follow the signs or directions, or take the right means of transport. We most probably would never have made it. Ultimately we might have, but it would have been after getting lost and maybe getting into trouble with the police or something.

Our walk with God is pretty much the same. We need to hear from Him, commune with Him, follow His directions[5] if we are to make any meaningful progress, indeed if we want to fulfill our destiny. Recall that He formed us, foreknew us and predestined us.[6][7] So He is in a good stead to direct us and lead us through the maze of life. Recall that His word is a lamp to our feet and a light to our path. [5] Our path to where exactly? He knows, so pay attention. It will only pay us in the long run because, this way, we are most certain of our destination.

Ours is a destination of peace, joy, anointing, health, prosperity, abundance, increase, fruitfulness.[8] Don't wonder where I got this from; look through His word and you'll see it splayed from Genesis to Revelation.

---

[5] Psalm 119:105

[6] Romans 8:9

[7] Ephesians 2:10

[8] Deuteronomy 11:8-22

8 August, 2012

TRAFFIC LIGHTS, MOVING WITH GOD AND NOT THE CROWD

Pris and I were coming back from late evening shopping; there was the need to buy some stuff we needed for the house since we had just arrived Nigeria from London. On our way to the house, we used the road by the Federal Secretariat in Abuja so we could connect the expressway that leads home. Since it was late we did not encounter heavy traffic. As we approached one of the traffic lights it was red, so we stopped.

The vehicle ahead of ours sped off, not seeming to notice that the light was red. Other vehicles sped past us and the traffic lights as well. I looked at Pris and we began to wonder if the lights were broken and now permanently on the red display. This feeling was heightened by the fact that we had been out of town for a few weeks, and we were feeling like new arrivals who were unaware of goings on or changes. Just then another vehicle slowed down a bit but kept moving forward. At this time two other cars behind ours seemed to be maneuvering to get out of there and leave. All this while, the light remained red and it seemed like it was taking forever. Time seemed to have frozen and all the cars would overtake us and we'd be there forever only to find that the light was broken after all and permanently red. Then we would have made fools of ourselves by being obedient to broken lights.

I opened my mouth to share my thoughts with Pris when the lights turned amber, then green. Whew! We were good to go and so we did while discussing what had just happened. Imagine if we had run the red light? Because we stopped and waited it would seem others had the courage and imbibed the patience to do same. You know, at a point we thought the lights were broken simply because others were running the lights without any hesitation. So we were tempted to believe the lie and follow suit. As a matter of fact, we almost became deadened to what we considered proper.

Same applies to our Christian lives and the world. If we remain in certain circles long enough we might begin to accept unacceptable things as the norm because we have been deadened.[9][10] In today's world, homosexuality is okay and termed 'gay' while Sodom and Gomorrah are recorded to have been destroyed because of same. [11][12] Think of other examples such as premarital sex being seen as "*having fun*", stealing looked upon as "*hammer*ing", telling lies as "*being sharp*". I am sure there are many more which should drive us to being cautious.

No wonder He tells us to take heed who thinks he is standing lest he fall.[13][14] A constant keeping in touch with the Word of God as our standard is sure to keep us hedged in.[15] Be cautious not to run the **"STOP"** lights of God's precepts; they are still working.

---

9   1 Corinthians 15:33

10 Hebrews 3:12-14

11 Genesis 19:4, 24

12 Jude 1:7

13 Deuteronomy 4:9 (Indeed the whole chapter warns to take heed)

14 1 Corinthians 10:12,13

15 Psalm 119:9

14 August, 2012

BUSINESS CLASS

I had to get an early flight to Lagos from Abuja to meet up with the timing on my engagements. Initially I had gotten an economy class ticket which was slated for noon; there was a paucity of flights because of the crisis of the aviation sector. But there was an urgent need for me to get to Lagos in time, so I kept scouting for a 7am flight. I did find one with space but it was in business class as all the economy tickets had been booked. So I spoke with my Executive Director who gave the nod for me to upgrade my flight ticket to business, which I did.

On getting to the airport to check in, the first visible thing was the long queue at the check-in counter. Looking closely, I saw that it was the economy line. So I went to the business class check-in counter which did not have too many people on queue; really there was no one on queue I as I found it. From the other queue I heard murmurs alluding to me getting preferential treatment and not joining the long queue, and someone said in retort to the protester, "That is the business class section". When we finally boarded, I noticed that there were only eight seats for business class on that aircraft which had two people per row. The rest of the aircraft had three people per row yet we were in the same aircraft.

Another thing is that this airline usually would not provide any in-flight meals for free; you would have to pay for anything you had in the economy cabin. But in business class I was offered a free meal and not just a snack. This is in addition to having a comfortable seat with more leg room. But to be there one had to pay more. I could have paid less and the cheaper fare would have afforded me the cheaper ride only. But because I paid the price I got what I got with its attendant benefits.

Reflecting on this, we could liken it to our Christian race. Many do not want to "pay the price," preferring to take the cheaper route such as a marginal prayer life, no tithes, living as they please, etc. This simply keeps such as one living on much less than the promised provisions of God. If we would get to the "Promised Land" of our destinies, the price of absolute obedience must be paid.

But once you have paid and gotten in, you will take the business class seat and you'll be given all that comes with it. So, leaving all that lies behind, we should press on towards to prize.[16]

---

[16] 2 Corinthians 5:7

24 July, 2012

EXERCISE YOUR FAITH –
DON'T LIMIT GOD

This was the afternoon of Friday, 24th August, 2012. It was a lovely day in all respects and I had so much to praise God for. This was especially so since a major breakthrough had come my way. I was on my way to meet a friend whose establishment had engaged the services of our firm. He'd just broken the news to me that two outstanding payments of ours were now ready. Such great news, a testimony that deserves a book dedicated to it! As a result of this news I was rushing off to meet him in the office where he was processing the payments.

On getting there, I realized that parking space was a problem; the parking lot was full. Not only was the lot jammed with vehicles, I had not come out with a driver; so I had to find parking space myself. Not a pleasant prospect. Then I heard a still small voice of the Holy Ghost asking me to test my faith. He asked me to drive on and move towards the more crowded part, that I would find space. He asked me how close to the entrance I wanted and I said in my heart that I wanted to be quite close to the gate so as to have a short walk in and out. He said, "Drive on then". You bet I did. Sounds easy, right? Well, inching up, indeed there was parking space. "Lovely," I thought. The voice said, "Push your faith further; go forward." Now what was the prospect of finding another space just as the one I was just giving up? Almost nil. But I pressed on. There now, I did find another spot in the crowded parking lot. He asked me if I wanted to move closer still, exercise my faith more. And I did, left this new space and drover further up, closer to the gate and... you've guessed it, there was another space closer to the place I wanted to be. All these opportunities (spaces) appeared where I needed and wanted them to be.

The Holy Spirit still asked me if I wanted to move closer to the gate. And at this point, I said, no thanks. I could see the gate and there was no need pushing this further since I was already reasonably close. I had learnt the lesson. I thought, "God is faithful, interested in everything that concerns me, including parking space." So I took that spot and alighted, and as I walked forward, behold another space so close to the entrance it could only have be pre-ordained by God. The Spirit spoke to me again saying, "The lesson is for you to exercise your faith. To the extent that you exercise it you will see unparalleled growth."

Oh, thank you Father because the 'faith walk' is powerful and I wish to walk in it. The 'sight walk' is ever so appealing yet limiting, and greatly so!

So let us walk by faith, and not sight.[17] Exercise your faith muscles and you can only come out in top shape. There is nothing to lose except your unbelief.

---

[17] Deuteronomy 6:30

16 September, 2012

I WANT TO ENJOY BEING IN GOD'S PRESENCE AND NOT JUST ENTER IT OUT OF A SENSE OF DUTY OR DISCIPLINE.[18]

Of course, there are several reasons to seek God's presence and want to be in it. There are lots of advantages in belonging to God – prosperity, solutions, health, and even the sense of doing what God wants. But beyond all this, there is the pure delight of just belonging to the Lord, and basking in the beauty of His presence.

I am prompted to put up the heading but no experience to back it up. In keeping with the spirit of the book, I encourage you to write this chapter for yourself. Adapt your own experience and let us see where the Spirit will lead with it.[19]

---

[18] 2Thessalonians 3:5
[19] Malachi 3:8-17

27 December, 2012

TRUST – GIVE IN – LET GO

"Mammy give me my lollipop...!" sobbed my son. "Chizi, what is the matter?" I asked my two-year-old son who was now sobbing profusely. In his language he then narrated to me how his mum had asked for his lollipop and he would not give it.

I thought about it and asked him if Mama could buy him a lollipop, and he nodded in the affirmative. I also asked if she had ever bought him some in the past. Another nod. Then I told him to relax. If she could buy him the lollipop he wanted, there was no harm in sharing the tiny one he had left.

Thinking of it, I realize we often do the same to God. We hoard our time, talents, forgiveness, tithes, resources, etc, from Him.[20] Yet what He asks of us is so little

---

[20] Romans8:31-33

compared to what He has given, gives and can give.[21] He is an awesome God who can do more than we can ever ask or imagine. He's done it all for us, given us all things and only asks very little of us in comparison. It is time to trust and obey; it's time to give, not just a little but our all.

---

21 James 4:8

16 January, 2013

ASK AND YOU SHALL HAVE IT

I was in the office and she walked in to go over some documents. As she was leaving, she said she liked my unit; and that it was cool to always travel, come to the office at odd times and leave whenever you felt like it. I was not bound by the 8am-6pm rules and seemed to be having fun. I smiled and told her that my prayer for her was to be moved to work with me so she too could 'enjoy' all the privileges and glamour attached to my 'office'. We laughed and she left.

Less than a month thereafter, my boss suggested that she work with my unit, and I gladly obliged. Shortly afterwards, we were off to Lagos on a business trip, attending one meeting after another and barely stopping to catch a breath or a bite. We had not even checked into the hotel, and by 9pm we suspended all activities to grab a bite. At dinner, my boss asked this colleague of mine how her first day with us in my unit had been so far? She said it was hectic. We both laughed and told her that this was only a tip of the iceberg. The next day, we were meant to go back to Abuja, but something came up and we flew to Accra, Ghana, to take a few meetings. By evening, we were to have a dinner meet with some prospective clients and the day ended by 2am or so. The lady (my colleague) was no longer smiling. The glint she had begun the day with had left her eyes and she made some confessions: "We in Abuja (she was referring to other staff) just see you guys come to work, strut into and out of the office at any time, travel always and stay at nice hotels, and we did not know the really hard work you do". All they had been seeing was the glamour and not the loads of work that accompanied the glamour they saw and craved for.

A similar thing happens to us in our walk with God. He asks us to draw near and He'll draw near to us, so we should seek Him out even though He is always with us.[22] So we see people who actively seek Him, who pay the price and keep vigil with Him while we snore and sleep (Christ has paid the price so don't think I am referring to righteousness by self effort); these people are soaked in the Word. They seem to have all the peace, wisdom,

---

[22] Philippians 2:12,13

calm, joy, and everything going for them. So we envy them rather than working out our salvation.[23] We even misunderstand them, rather than running our race and diligently looking to the Author and Finisher of our faith; rather than or building our faith and letting Him who rewards those who diligently seek Him perform same wonders in our lives, we just envy, wish and gossip about these blessed people and their blessings.[24][25]

Let us all run this race that is set before us with our eyes on the prize, knowing and walking in that knowledge.

---

23 Hebrews 11:6

24 Hebrews 12:12

25 Mathew 5:16

4 February, 2013

PAY THE PRICE

"I'm sorry, but the bill is $10 to drop you off at the hotel," the car hire attendant said to me.

"But it is right behind this hotel," I responded. "You can see it is a walking distance."

"Okay, we'll charge you GH☐10".

"That's too much money to drop me off at such a short distance. I'll walk instead."

And walk I did, pulling my bag along the pedestrian walkway. All her attempts to get me to pay such a ridiculous sum had failed.

As I walked, I thought to myself how often we pay a higher price for convenience rather than take the hard route. The walk was short, good for my health; besides, I could take a shower once I was lodged at the hotel.

Same happens in our walk with God. Jesus was offered the opportunity to take the route of convenience and bow to the devil and gain all the kingdoms of the world. But He chose to walk to the cross to establish the kingdom of God instead. In your work, home and endeavors, do you traverse the route of convenience which is more costly, or do you take the hard road which eventually leads to refinement?

General Comment

We compartmentalize our lives often and live the office life, the home life, the church life, etc. It should not be so. The influence of God on our lives should permeate every sphere of our existence. Our light and lives should so shine amongst men that they see...and glorify our Father in Heaven.[26]

I am only trying to tie my regular daily experience to God and my walk in this life. I am certain you can fit your name, your story, your world, into this sphere of stories and ultimately into God's word toward our daily living.

---

[26] Luke 6:14

23 January, 2013

CAN YOU GIVE WHAT YOU DO NOT HAVE?

"We shall soon be showing you some of our safety features aboard this aircraft," said the voice of the airhostess over the speaker. Then they got to the part where they said, "In the event of sudden loss of cabin pressure, masks like these will automatically drop. Pull the masks toward you and put it over your face like this. The act of pulling the mask will release the flow of oxygen..." Then she said, "....put on your mask first before attempting to assist anyone else!!!" (emphasis mine).

I hear this on every flight, but it was only this time I began to wonder why it had to be so. If my child were beside me, or a loved one, the intent would be to make sure they were safe first before seeing to my own safety. The child would be helpless without me, right? They might suffocate and die if I did not act quickly. Wait a minute, the thought continued. What happens in such a situation is that there is loss of oxygen and so the brain is starved of same. This makes the person to become unconscious because the brain will shut down if it lacks oxygen to go on. And if you are in that state, you are of no use to anyone – even yourself – so you are likely to perish alongside the loved one you hoped to save.

This meant that, if you were to quickly put on your mask, you would stay conscious and be in the position to assist those in need, in this case your child. It made me think further, "If you did not have life, would you have given the help which translates to life?" You think about it.

Christ tells us that, out of the abundance of our heart the mouth speaks.[27] And a Latin adage says, *"Nemo dat quod non habet"* – nobody gives what he does not have.

Invariably we give from what we have. What else is interesting is that we are promised an outpouring of blessings from the storehouse of heaven, giving us from what they have.[28] To Abraham God said that he would be blessed to become a blessing, again a giving that

---

[27] Malachi 3:10
[28] Genesis 12:2

comes from what you have.[29] Jesus often went alone to pray, and when He came down from the mountain, He taught, healed, comforted, provided, led, guided and so on, and so forth. And He tells us that He does what He's seen the Father doing.[30] In spending time alone with God, seeking His face, looking unto Him always, Jesus got something which He passed on to us.

How many times have we been in situations where we could do nothing, give nothing because we had nothing to give. We could not comfort, exhort, rebuke, correct or feed the hungry in situations of need because we were empty. We fail to spend time with God, in study and prayer, and so we do not have the weapons or equipment required to tackle the situation, even stave off the devil. Jesus could. After 40 days in the wilderness, He gave the tempter the Word (of God) for every arrow of temptation the devil shot at him. Apply this to any part of your life as you may. If you refuse to save, you will have nothing at retirement or the rainy day. If you do not study, you will not be able to give your examiners the answers they require of you. We could go on and on citing examples.

---

[29] John 3:30
[30] Mark 2:17

There is a choice to be made today; what will it be? Will you build on the rock, or on sand? Will you sow in order to reap? Will you gather, will you...will you...? It is your choice. God, on the other hand, has chosen to bless us.

25 January, 2013

I'M SANE, THEY KNOW NOTHING

He pulled out of nowhere and almost slammed into my car. "This guy must have bought his driver's license to be driving like that," was the thought that flashed through my mind. Then he suddenly applied the brakes, trafficated and went left missing my bumper by a hairbreadth. I had done some hard braking as well, and luckily there was no vehicle behind mine. "Another learner unleashed on unsuspecting road users," I thought. It did not end there. Taxis and commercial bus drivers seemed to be in a race to bash or be bashed, and I was tempted to think I was the only one who was sane.

Oh, there we go again! So I sped up and overtook the fellow, cutting him off while poking a finger at my head to as though asking, "Are you mad? *You don craze?*" After the small drama, I drove off and realized I had just behaved like the people of whom I had been critical of all day long. But I was not going to keep on that path, so

I slowed down to apologize with more hand signs. I got a hoot (I was unsure, but hope he meant I was forgiven), took it in good faith and drove off.

Very often we think we are better than "these people". We will not drink to stupor like "those guys" or sleep around like "her". It is easy to be critical and think we cannot be like "them" because we keep looking at their shortcomings. We fail to realize that we too have failings that are sore in the consideration of "others" even if we might be working on them. Not only do we fall, we often end up in so much mess, yet God takes us back once we repent. So thinking we stand, let us stay on alert or we might fall flat on our faces.[31] We ought to pray for those who do wrong and not treat them with disgust (*diss them*). After all, the sick do need medical attention and not rejection; Jesus said so himself.[32] Even our enemies are to receive our prayers and blessings not lashing and vengeance.[33] Think about it, "...all have sinned" [32], not some but all. If you say you say you are exempt then you make God a liar. Let us give mercy to gain mercy in abundance, taking the word of God seriously and not remaining in a fallen state.

---

[31] 1 Corinthians 10:12,13

[32] Romans 12:19-21

[33] Romans 3:23

1 February, 2013

WATCH FORWARD

We were heading to Mohammadu Buhari Way to reach the bank for an urgent transaction. It was almost 4pm, their closing time. I noticed the driver was paying much attention to the rear-view mirror. Looking ahead I saw a car pulling out into the highway, and the driver seemed not to be paying much attention. *"Pally, look front!"* I firmly exclaimed to mine. He looked up, blared his car horn, hit the brakes hard and narrowly averted a collision with the other vehicle. Having returned his attention to the road ahead enabled us avert the car crash.

However, no sooner had we passed this near miss than he returned his gaze and attention to the rear view-mirror once again, obviously seething and watching the car that had very nearly endangered our lives. *"Ol' boy, face ya front! Make you dey look ya front!"* were my next comments to him, drawing his attention to the road ahead. We had approached a major intersection and he needed to pay full attention of course, else we would be endangering ourselves and others as well.

All this got me thinking that Jesus had asked us to daily pick up our cross and follow.[1] Paul admonished that we leave what is behind and press forward, ...looking to Jesus who begins and ends our faith.[2] So very often we get carried away with our past or the goings-on around us, that we fail to keep our eyes on Jesus. These things, problems as they often are, loom so large they occupies us completely. We keep our sights there, oblivious to what is ahead, who is ahead, our Master Jesus, and we crash and burn. It may be children, church activities or other things that occupy us, so much so that we lay aside the cross to carry those burdens. The rear-view mirror is small for a reason, while the windscreen is large and fitted with wipers as well being assisted with headlamps.

Peter walked on water so long as he had his sight on Jesus; but the moment his gaze moved to the *waves,* he began to sink. Do not be so focused on the *rear-view mirror* of near misses, the madness of others, activities, a lost loved one, a broken heart, the past, and much more. Do not be so focused on these things that you do not pay attention to what is ahead of you through the large windscreen of the Word. Please keep your eye on Jesus the Author and Finisher of our faith. May God remain visibly present in our lives. Amen!

11 November, 2012

TAKE HEED, STAY SHARP, STAY ALIVE

As we drove to church in the morning, I was enjoying the drive, the music, the scenery, and the fact that I was reunited with my family after a long time of travelling. I did not notice that the speedometer had gone past 120km/h and the speed warning light was indicating same with the alarm beeping. Now it was easy to ignore all the signs and carry on after I had noticed it. But that was not a safe speed to be at (the needle was on 160km/hr, approximately 99 miles per hour).

You can imagine what could have happened, the consequences, and so on. So how did I get to that point in the first place? Simply by not paying attention. Same applies to our walk with Christ, you know? That is why we are told to take heed, we who think we are standing, lest we fall.[34] When you miss the little things – it might

---

[34] 1 Corinthians 10:12,13

be as little as not studying the word or praying, watching the wrong movie, hanging on to the wrong relationships, averting fellowship, the list goes on – we could readily be setting up stumbling blocks for ourselves. Should there be a sudden 'power outage', you could trip up against any of these things and fall badly. There is no telling what injuries may result, or the scars they will leave, assuming we survive the fall.

So, take heed, stay sharp and stay alive in Christ.

10 February, 2013

YOU MEAN HE DID THAT WITH MY GIFT?

It was a pair of leather boots I had bought while on a trip abroad, and my, they were lovely! They had this dusty look like you had just come from a dusty site with all the dirt on your boots. These were a rugged pair designed to give a brother a rugged yet pristine look. Actually, I bought two pairs; don't ask me why, but they ended up as gifts to my friends shortly upon my return.

After a while I saw one of them wearing the boots proudly, but they seemed to have a strange luster. Looking closely I noticed my friend had put a generous amount of polish on the shoes to even out the dusty look, in order to get a normal *shine* on the boots. This was an attempt at getting a soldier's shine. Oh boy, he was not aware of how to care for this pair. All it needed were shoe protectors. Neither did he understand and appreciate the rugged beauty of the initial color. As a result, he attempted to make it resemble everyone else's. He tried to make the gift conform to what was common. But this was an uncommon gift, one unique to him with a different way to manage it.

On the other hand, I never saw my second friend wear the boots. What had he done with my gift? Had he stowed it away? Perhaps he too was wondering what kind of *dirty* boots he had received from me?

I must tell you that I felt concerned, disappointed, worried, upset at how my gifts had been used. If only the first fellow had asked me how to manage the leather. If they had both asked to know more about the gifts, I would have gladly obliged them with the information. They sure would have gotten the best out of the boots.

Just as in either case, we too have been given unique gifts by God. He really wants us to make the move of it, to maximize the use of our gifts. We are not to hide it away, nor are we to use them the way we feel is best. Ask the Giver and let Him guide you on how to optimize them.

26 September, 2012

I TRUST GOD BUT...?

We were in a cable car in Sentosa, Singapore, and we were really enjoying it. It was my first experience on such a ride high up there, and really scary. The thought of hanging on a cable and being moved over such a height brought all kinds of thoughts to my mind. What if the mechanism stalled and we were stuck midway to the next station? What if the cable cut and we fell or there was some form of natural disaster and we all fell out? Looking out, I saw other cable cars, which brought some comfort. "We are not alone, so these guys must know what they are doing," I thought. "It will all work out to be a great experience." Indeed it turned out to be so. The ride back was with less trepidation; in fact, with none at all.

God who made the universe has called us to trust Him because He has purposed what we are to do in this life[35]. Our lives are in His hands. He makes all things turn out for our good. But we are afraid to trust. It is easier for us to believe we'll be paid a salary but are not so sure of receiving the answer to a prayer. We believe we will get to the office in the morning but not confident that God can give us a promotion; we think our boss is responsible for that. We make Him too small, doubt so much, when we need only trust and allow Him to do the work in our lives.

---

35 Ephesians 2:10

2010

MAKURDI-OBOLLO-AWKA

I was up to an early start, driving through many towns and villages from Makurdi to Obollo Afor, onward to Awka in Anambra State. The road was bridled with potholes and required the utmost attention of both the government and the drivers plying the road.

At some point there were two cars ahead of mine also weaving and maneuvering to dodge the potholes. I found myself following their lead and depending on their decisions in order to dodge these craters myself. When they went left, I did. Any direction they took I followed, believing that, since they were in front of me they could see what lay ahead and make timely and accurate decisions to avert the potholes. I was wrong! I found myself falling into so many holes it was amazing. There were times I found myself facing an oncoming vehicle although sometimes they made good calls that worked for me as well.

So, I decided to do my own thing. Either overtake them or give them a wide berth so I could clearly see what was ahead of me.

Very often we pace ourselves by how others are living. We gauge our spirituality by what they say or think. What we call success is what they call it, and we lose sight of the road ourselves and often fall into the pits that they fall into. We ought to gauge this life by our Master and let Him be our pacemaker.[36]

---

36 Hebrews12:2

4 May, 2013

A LIVING BIBLE

Yesterday I saw a man live out his faith. He was the Bible I read and meditated on for most of the evening.

He worked in a high-stress environment, really demanding if you ask me. And on this day he had to deal with me (my firm), various government agencies, his colleagues, subordinates and superiors and we all wanted our way. We were opinionated, felt we were right, expressed our aggression towards him and, to say the least, tried to demean, insult and lord it over him. But he remained focused, never raised his voice, listened, explained, kept to the plan and targets to be achieved. Emotions ran high that day, egos were bruised, insults were slung across the phone, threats were issued but this gentleman stuck to facts and remained comported.

He did not let all these things sway him from what was to be achieved. His patience, even when emphasizing the 'truths' of the operation, were factually passed across without his losing his cool. If I were in his shoes, there is no telling what I could have done. But he maintained a composed disposition. He embodied Christ, as far as I am concerned, and I'm proud he chose to remain a part of the cloud of witnesses; God bless him.

We ought to do right, not always for ourselves but for the sake of those to whom we might end up being the only Bible that they ever get to read to encounter Christ[37].

---

[37] 2 Corinthians 3:2-4

18 June, 2013

LIGHT ON A HILL

He introduced me to his colleague who retorted, "...but I have seen you before." He went on to add, "Were you at Heathrow Airport last week? You were wearing a white shirt and brown khaki pants?" I replied, "Yes, sir, you are correct". Indeed I had been seen and this event took place sometime the previous year. More recently, I took a trip by road and we had an incident with the Federal Road Safety Corps (FRSC) stationed in Abaji in the FCT. Three days later, over 400 kilometers away in a fuel station in Umuahia, someone I had never seen before walked up to me and asked, "Did the Road Safety men give you back your camera the other day?" I was taken aback but responded in the affirmative and thanked him for his concern.

Still on that incident with the FRSC; while I was trying to get my seized camera, I was taken to a gentleman who chose to assist. At the end of it, he asked if I knew who he was. I told him that he looked a bit familiar. "Let me not pretend, you worship with me at CAFON. I know you, your wife and your child." "Oh boy, what if I had done something awry or silly or lost my cool while all this had been going on?" was my thought. Which brings me to yet another trip to Calabar early this month. The day after my arrival, I asked the fellow I was working with to take me round car stands to make an enquiry. He did. That evening I got a call from one of my close friends who lives in Abuja. He asked me, *"Pally, you don come back town?" "No bros, I never return,"* came my reply. *"Pesin, ... call me say im see you for car stand for Calabar...."* Yes, you know it, I had been sighted again. I never got to meet this person who saw me, nor did the person stop to say hi. All through my one-week stay in Calabar I did not encounter a familiar face.

Imagine for a moment as I undertook these journeys I felt I was far away from where anyone could see me and decided to live carelessly. Perhaps I lost my cool while dealing with the FRSC matter or picked a fight in Calabar, done something funny in London, you name it. Surely, someone somewhere would have seen it and taken note, and I wonder what effect it would have had on the person? Will you be a source of light or a dampening influence?[38] I am not in any way advocating some crazy self-consciousness; that is undue pressure that could negate the grace of God, and man cannot cope with it. Just remember that Christ is in you. He is the light. And that light shines in you and through you. And that light is on a hill, it cannot stay hidden.

Simply put, live for Christ. It won't matter who's watching. Because you are living for the one who has called us, living in His presence, daily taking up your cross to follow. He'll do the rest, distribute His light in you, letting it shine through you that the Father may be glorified.

---

38 Matthew 5:13-15

27 June, 2013

GAZE UPON...MORE AND BE TAKEN IN

I was missing home. There was a myriad of issues to deal with and my head was popping in all directions. This was stressful. In the process of getting some of the things I needed from my phone, I accidentally went to my pictures. There she was, my last daughter, a beautiful smile on her face, holding on to her cot. I scrolled to the next photo and there they were; her older brother and sister hugging each other. I scrolled... and scrolled looking through photo upon photo of my family and basking in the memories of each of those moments. In fact, I was caught up in it. There was a warmth that flowed from within. At that moment I was raptured, shut in a time capsule and all else fell away. A sense of comfort came over me and I felt much better.

It then hit me. When we are faced with 'Life,' who do we gaze upon, who do we look to? What pictures can still our minds, calm our aching hearts, restore hope and give us strength? I realized that looking at Jesus, looking to Him, would have a similar effect on us as did those photographs on me. As a matter of fact, it will do more; restore our souls and lead us to still waters. When the storms of life are raging around us and it seems we are walking or sinking in it, we should focus on Jesus and not the storm. The trials will come, the enemy will attack; be it through a co-worker, a boss, siblings, business, you name it. But they will flee in all directions, fall in the pit they have dug while you will have your table prepared with a feast laid out in the midst of it all. Simply keep your eyes on Jesus.

One more thing: recall what He has done in your life, anything at all. It is your testimony, an anchor point. If he did it then He can do it again and more. He is in charge, does not change and is always the same. Gaze upon Him and come away with more than a testimony. Come away being more like Him.[39]

---

[39] Mathew 14:28-30

28 July, 2013

ROCK THE BOAT

The gangway could not be lowered on the portside, so we had to access the ship via the starboard. This implied a boat ride. We got in cautiously into this engine-propelled canoe which bounced precariously on the waves. And off we went, sitting as still as we could manage, all trying to look calm. No one wanted to make sudden moves because it was sure to rock the boat. And rocking this piece of hewn-out wood, we would all be tossed into the sea. We were exposed, at the mercy of anything and everything. No one wanted the boat rocked, at least not I. We were hoping to disembark in one piece.

I think we pretty much have walked through life that way. If I knew how to swim perhaps it would not have been such a scary thing. Who knows, if it were a bigger vessel, like the one we were about to board, we would not have noticed any of these dangers. In life, we wish we had the right connections, more money, did not have to depend on anyone, could fend off fiends and a whole lot more. There are so many things that we should like to have as we traverse this sea of life on our little crafts. Yet Jesus has offered us himself. He is a life raft, the connection we need, a life jacket, that big vessel. He is All. With Him in our lives, the boat can rock as it likes, we know we are safe. Come on, this is the Guy that walked on water and calmed storms.

We no longer have to live in fear, or a less fulfilled life, because we have Jesus. We can now enjoy the voyage, the beautiful expanse of water, the bouncing waves, and not cling to our benches in fear. He has come to set us free from fear, depression, unforgiveness...you name it. He has done this so that we can have life to the full. Give it all to him and it won't matter anymore even if the boat were rocked; He is our anchor.

8 July, 2013

GETTING AHEAD, A ROUNDABOUT

The drive home each evening was not exactly something to look forward to because of the heavy traffic. It was often so heavy that some 'wise guys' would drive against oncoming traffic in a bid to get ahead. What they didn't reckon was that, at the point they tried to rejoin the regular traffic flow, they were obstructing traffic in all directions. So often they were the cause of the bad traffic situation they so often tried to 'beat'.

We become nasty to those who hurt us, resentful and spiteful, and talk wrong about those who have spread rumors about us. Often we pay back in the same coin what treatment we perceive we've received. This contributes to the 'traffic jam' of continued cycles of hurt, pain, resentment...wrong! If only we would follow the wisdom of the Master, be kind to those who hurt us, give a cup of water to a thirsty enemy, speak kindly about those who speak vile of us. Just as a doctor would treat a patient, if we would treat such people, then we would ease the 'flow of traffic'. It may not be as free as the highway, but then we would not be contributing to the clogs.

It most likely would go unnoticed and unappreciated by most, but not by God. He sees what's done in secret and rewards us accordingly.

1, October, 2013

GOING ON EVERYONE
ELSE'S ASSUMPTION

I needed some cash and stopped at the ATM along Marian Road in Calabar. It boasts about 6 machines and attracts a crowd of users. On this occasion (as had been on many others) there were quite a number of people awaiting their turns at various machines. As I approached I noticed that two of the stalls were vacant yet no one seemed to be making a move to occupy those booths.

Asking the people around, they told me that they came there and noticed that no one went there. So they ended up queuing up at the other stalls assuming that those machines were out of service or could not dispense cash. So I went to one of the empty stalls and tried. Behold, it paid me! Immediately there was a queue formed awaiting my vacation of the booth. I then asked again if anyone had tried the empty, abandoned one by my side and they chorused "No". "Why not try it?" I quipped. Someone did and it paid.... Another queue? You bet.

Imagine how many times we hang on to the opinion of the crowd and follow, not minding to crosscheck. It happens in the churches, schools, and everywhere in society. And this crowd opinion is not necessarily accurate. In our Christian lives we ought not to go with the crowd. We ought to crosscheck doctrine against the word[40].

Yes, and it does pay.

---

[40] 1 Thessalonians 5:20-22

15 October, 2013

HE SAID... JUST DO IT

It was the evening before the Sallah celebration; he called me and directed me to go pick up a goat from Francis on site. An exciting preposition this was for me. So the next morning I went for the pick-up.

On getting to site and asking the gateman where I could find Francis, I got a confusing shock; he did not know who I was referring to. I called a colleague of mine in the city office and she was not sure either. She said she knew of a Patrick and gave me his number to call. The gateman also knew who Patrick was so I called him, thinking within me that I might not have heard my boss right. Unfortunately, Mr Patrick would not pick the call. At this point, I had begun to doubt what I had been instructed to do. But the *bossman* had been clear, I heard him, asked him to re-affirm the name in the course of our discourse and ...I think he had said Francis.

"Why not call the source of your instruction?" a part of me asked. I hesitated, not wanting to come off as inattentive or ineffective or anything of the sort that could give a boss concerns as to my effectiveness. But I went ahead and called. His response was an affirmation of what I already knew; it was Francis I was to meet. This was an elucidation as to whom I was to meet, a grounding in my mission. Francis had been recently deployed to site, and boy, was I relived! The doubts had been cleared from my mind. I had been on the right track all along and was working with the right information.

There are times we fall into doubt – doubt of our calling, a revelation, prophesy about us, that our prayer request will be answered, and the list goes on[41]. Like Peter when Jesus asks to come to Him walking on the water, let us step out of the boat and walk. Along the way we may experience things that make us doubt this calling (and His calling is sure)[42]. We often look to the *waves* and end up sinking. But calling to Him as I did my boss will surely re-affirm the call. Oh, He'll surely reach out and pull you up.

---

[41] Habakkuk 2:2-4

[42] 2 Timothy 1:9

2012

SATELLITE NAVIGATION

He knew the destination; at least he had the address and we were at our take-off point. All he had to do was impute the address into the satnav and it would guide us to our destination. This he did and we commenced our journey to Heathrow Airport, Terminal 3. As we moved along the voice would give directions like, "intersection ahead, turn left" or "xxx street ahead, continue for twenty yards then...." We had adequate instruction every step of the way.

Another thing was that the display showed the roads in relation to where we were. It pointed us in the way to go. What it did not do was to us show us the destination. It took us through the journey, acted as our guide at every point so we did not miss our way. Even when we did miss our way, it provided an alternate route which brought us back on track. We lost time, yes, because the alternates were often longer, but we did get back on track and headed to our destination ultimately.

Pretty much like following our Lord we know in part, prophecy in part, we know the destination: Heaven. We have only to follow His prompting and guidance. It is absolute reliance on His direction. Even when we lose our way we can trust He'll re-direct and re-route us and take us ultimately to our destination.

Our journey continues even as the book ends, each experience enriching in its own right if only we could notice it. I guess that is also one of the reasons why he says "..be still and know that I am God.."[43]

---

43 Psalm 46:10

ABOUT THE AUTHOR

For over a decade, Collins Nwosu has travelled quite a lot, locally and internationally. This has afforded him the opportunity of varied experiences.

In addition, his life as a Christian, husband, father, supervisor and employee has allowed him some of the unique perspectives he shares with us in Road Series.

He currently lives in Abuja, Nigeria, with his wife and children, still traveling and garnering even more experiences.